How to Harness the
Power of the Moon

with

Archangel Haniel

What are the four healing cycles of the moon?

Moon rituals to heal the soul

HOW TO HARNESS THE POWER OF THE MOON

WITH

ARCHANGEL HANIEL

What are the four healing cycles of the moon?

Moon rituals to heal the soul

Z.Z. RAE

Other Books by Z.Z. Rae

- Your Voice Your Choice: The Value of Every Woman
- Ties of the Heart: How to recover from Divorce and Breakups (A 12 step-by-step healing process)
- I Want to be a Unicorn (Why Unicorns are Real and You can be One

Angel Guidance Series

- Angel Guidance for Wealth (Abundant Living for Everyone)
- Angel Guidance for Dreams (Your Dreams explained by the Angels)
- Angel Guidance for Inner Healing (Heal your Heart, Soul, and Mind with the Angels)
- Angel Guidance for Creativity (Unlock Your Gift)
- Angel Guidance for Peace (Allow life's burdens to fade)
- Angel Guidance for Joy (Raise your Vibrations)
- Angel Guidance for Energy Healing (Aligning your beliefs with your desires)
- Angel Guidance for Awakening Spiritual Gifts (Uncover your natural ability)

Spiritual Tools

- How to Work with Archangels: (Guidance from archangels for abundance, healing, spiritual wisdom, and more.)

- How to Declutter with Archangel Jophiel (How to Relieve Stress, Anxiety, and Clutter From Your Life)
- How to Work with Archangel Michael (How do I know my life's purpose?)
- How to Find What's Missing with Archangel Chamuel (There's nothing lost in the Kingdom)

Magical Mermaid Messages

- Magical Mermaid Messages on Abundance (How to manifest money with the law of abundance)
- How to Manifest a Soulmate (with a little help from the mermaids)
- How to Manifest a Soulmate Journal (A journal to attract your soulmate)

Books by Natasha House

Grace Alive Series

Christian Romance

- Grace Alive
- Grace Unbroken

Rebirth of the Prophesy Series

Sci-fi Romance

- Fatal Alien Affection
- Fatal Alien Attraction

The Jade Series

Epic Fantasy

- The Vullens' Curse
- The Deities' Touch
- The Vision Stone

Super Hero Princess Series

Middle grade/Young Adult

- Zara

Non-Fiction

- How to KEEP Writing Your Book
- Illustrated Sermons for Youth or Adults
- Grace Speaks

For the sensitive ones

Intro

The moon called to me.

I've been interested in this subject for a while, but I never quite jumped in. As I thought about which archangel to work with next, Archangel Haniel smiled at me. I just knew.

It was time to harness the power of the moon.

I'd been getting these little nudges to look up stuff about the moon for quite some time, but now I finally had an excuse to put it all down.

Some weeks I'd have these crazy emotional days, and then later I'd talk to my friend, and she'd tell me, *"The moon was full."*

I'd often wonder if that was superstition, or if there truly was something to the moon doing crazy stuff to us.

It wasn't just the full moon, it was also the new moon—which was something altogether different.

I wanted to say, *"Moon, what are you doing to me? Leave me alone!"*

From what I've read, there isn't really scientific evidence to the moon impacting us, but as we know, science catches up with spirituality like way later. Look at the stuff spiritual leaders said 5,000 years ago, and you'll see how the world of science finally caught up.

I believe in the power of belief, and if you believe the moon stages can help you deal with emotional issues—it will work for you. I swear, there is something to this, because during stages of my cycles (or the moon doing her crazy stuff) I'd find different emotions arising.

Every woman out there will attest to these stages of their menstrual cycle. As I researched this, I found myself thankful for the information. I finally had something solid to look at.

As a teen, I remember crying about my emotional problems every month and not understanding why. No one ever really explained to me PMS, and I wish I would have known how to process my emotions when I was young. I pray not only you get something from this, but you can teach your kids and teens how to deal with the power of their emotions.

As I've researched for articles I've written, I was saddened by the amount of anxiety and depression in the world. I feel like learning stuff like this can help heal people's minds, hearts, and emotions.

What if understanding what's going on eases these mental disorders? Not to say that they completely go away, but I've found when I understand something about myself, it eases almost instantly.

I know this is a long intro, but bear with me. I am passionate about helping people emotionally. I look around the world, and I see how people can't seem to handle their emotions.

They smother them with a quick fix, and then wonder why they're not happy with their life. The media is shoved in our faces, and it forces us to dive into the world of fantasy, instead of sitting five minutes with ourselves to feel relief.

Sometimes we aren't allowing the four stages to roll through. Not that it's all women, because men have stages too, but from what I've learned, it's a bit different for men. It makes sense, because in most cultures the moon is known as a *she.* If we can understand these concepts, how much more conscious and aware will we be?

I'd say a lot. As you open yourself up to Archangel Haniel's messages, hear the kindness in her words. Although I had to study for this book, I asked her to use her words as I wrote what I learned. She has such a gentle energy, and I truly believe she wants to help women be empowered by these cycles.

How many of us feel degraded or *gross* during our menstrual cycle? In fact, PMS is made fun of, but what if we honored our body instead of shaming it?

Think about it—men get PMS too, it just looks different. While maybe women get weepier, men will grow angry. They also need to release and understand themselves.

As you honor your emotional stages, you'll grasp the power of harnessing the moon. I hope you enjoy Archangel Haniel's messages.

-Z.Z. Rae

<u>Note from the Author</u>

I write what I hear from the divine. Whether it comes from angels, fairies, mermaids, or a divine source. I let their words be authentic. As you dive into this book, have an open mind for the archangels to teach you. Every book I write changes me, and I hope it can bring you healing.

We never worship angels or pray to them, but we can receive help if we are open to it. I believe these angels want to help spread a message of love to everyone who is willing to open their hearts.

-Z.Z. Rae

Chapter 1: Who is Archangel Haniel?

Insert from: How to Work with Archangels

Archangel Haniel's name means:

Glory of God

Archangel Haniel keeps watch over the seventh, or Netzach, Sephirah (emanation of God's will) in the Kabbalah. This portion of the Sefirot characterizes overcoming our inside world, imagination, emotions, and intuition.

Humans' natural free will is marked by the Netzach Sephirah, and also represents resolve and stamina. It's the full expression of love here on Earth.

Archangel Haniel's Gifts

Higher Vision

Are you drawn to clairvoyance? Archangel Haniel can aid you in practicing your seeing abilities and intuition or other forms of revered feminine energy.

Full Moon Releasing

When the full moon is up, Haniel can be of assistance to help you heal and rid yourself of any old, toxic emotions. If you are dealing with womanly issues, Haniel can help with that too.

Spiritual Gifts

When you're learning to tap into your spiritual gifts, Haniel is a guidance into your inner world. Even though there is feminine energy coming from Haniel, men also can reap benefits from a connection to her—since men carry this type of energy as well. Just as men have feminine energy, women have male energy. Haniel brings awakening to inner wisdom and guidance for all.

Artists and Marriage

If you need help as an artist or in matters such as marriage or children, Haniel will assist you with your needs.

Color:

Pale Blue (Moonlight)

Crystals and Gemstones:

Rose Quartz, Pink Calcite, Chrysoprase, and Moonstone

Zodiac Sign:

Oversees all

Archangel Haniel in a Nutshell

- Higher Vision
- Full Moon Releasing
- Spiritual Gifts
- Artists and Marriage

Message from Archangel Haniel

Beautiful things are happening inside of you, little ones. I can see each thing like a precious, little bud about to bloom. Take heart that things are in motion for you in the right season and time.

I will help open your eyes to see beyond your natural abilities. Trust what you are sensing, feeling, seeing, hearing, tasting, smelling, and touching. You have great insight buried inside of you. Use your God-given talents to bring light into the world and further the cause of love and light.

Affirmation to Archangel Haniel

"Dear Archangel Haniel, thank you for awakening my intuition and helping me clearly see what I need to see. I release all past issues, and I thank you for helping me clear them."

Chapter 2: The Cycle

Let's start this off by saying, hi. (Laughs) So many times people think it's just plain out weird to talk to any of us angels—let alone an archangel. I'm rather down-to-earth with humans, because I understand their language in a way many other higher beings may not.

Not to say we are *higher* than you, because that is also a misconception. I won't go too far into that, but needless to say, you don't need to be weirded out.

When people think of me, they often think of the moon. While yes, the moon and I are deeply connected, I also help with a variety of things. The moon is an energy to help you let go on a monthly basis. If you study the science behind the moon cycles, they may tell you there is no significance to it with your emotions.

I beg to differ, only because of the beliefs carried from one generation to another. These beliefs carry the power to overcome deep emotional issues. When you harness the power of the moon during these cycles, you will feel many burdens shed over time.

That is why I want to get down with you about this. The moon will assist you, just as I will assist you. Think of the moon as your mother or sister, who wishes to guide you through things you have been avoiding.

If you are a woman, you understand the natural cycle of your body. You grasp that there are times of natural release, and if you fight that release, it only makes you more pent up.

What am I talking about?

Menstruation. If you want me to put it simply. Women have been shamed for this cycle for years, and it's even joked about by men and women alike. I want you to look at this cycle in a different way.

It is a time of cleansing. If you honor this time in your body, you can release any and all built up emotions.

People Joke About the Moon

They talk about how the full moon makes people crazy. There are legends and myths about it as well. If you search way back, the full moon could be looked at in a negative light.

This is the culture I want to change. Just like a woman's menstruation cycle is a time to let go of built up emotional baggage, so the full moon is a time to release. If you work with the energies of the moon, you'll find it much easier and less painful to go with the flow of those energies.

If you don't love, accept, and honor the natural release in yourself, it will only create more emotions to express in the future. People try to hide away from their emotional build ups. They let go in secret, which is okay to do, but they also repress it many times. Especially males.

I'm not here to pick on men, but they've been conditioned to repress their natural cycles. While their cycle of release is a tad different, women can help them connect to the *moon* side of them—or the feminine.

Everyone releases in different ways. Tears, venting, expressing. However it fits for them personally is perfectly fine. I love to help people with the ritual of release. I know some people don't like that word *ritual*, but all it means is a sacred routine for yourself.

Where can you go that feels safe? Find that sacred space, and create a little ritual that fits your personality. Here's a few ideas:

- Journal your thoughts
- Cry
- Punch a pillow
- Do something active
- Say a sacred prayer
- Meditate
- Visit a place in nature

There are a host of ways to release pent up emotions. What you feel best fits you—do that. If you find quietly retreating into a forest helps you let go, then do that. If you find venting by playing an active sport—do that. There is no one way to let the cycle take its course. It's what feels best to you.

Affirmation

I allow the cycle of release. I create sacred space and let go of old emotions.

Chapter 3: Sacred Space

Every one of you needs a sacred space. It doesn't have to be something too fancy. A simple blanket, mat, or corner of a room will do. Maybe your bedroom is your sacred space, or your heart creates a sacred space wherever you are. All of these are fine.

Creating sacred space helps you in a variety of ways. It lets your soul know it's safe to let go and release all the baggage it's acquired over the past month (or longer).

If you haven't allowed release to happen, you may experience pent-up emotions circling around and around. These emotions will find a way to release eventually. It can come in negative forms.

- Sickness
- Disease

- Emotional breakdowns
- Attracting poor situations
- Attracting negative relationships

If you do not acknowledge your body's natural signs, you may end up experiencing situations you don't enjoy. Your body gives you signs of what kinds of emotions are pent up.

The moon cycles can help you harness the energy every month (or daily) to release emotional baggage. This is why you have dreams. They help release pent-up emotions from your daily living.

Depending on how you process your feelings, you'll want to acquire a day-to-day routine of release. Some do not need this daily practice, while others do. This is not to say one is better than the other, but rather different.

27

Creating a safe space for yourself can help you release things before they manifest in your physical body or world. In the past, people didn't acknowledge the mind/body/heart connection, but many teachers now understand it. They see how holding a grudge impacts the stress levels in the body, so that it is prone to more sickness and disease.

Here's a few tips to release in your sacred space.

Tip 1

Get Comfy

When you are comfortable, you will remind yourself that you are at ease with whatever you wish to come out. You are free to express yourself, without fear of judgement from others. When you let your hair down, so to speak, you can connect with the part of yourself that wishes to be heard.

Tip 2

Listen

Listening to yourself is important. When your body starts to ache, ask it why. When your emotions are starting to seep out, tune in and acknowledge them. This is valuable in your sacred space, because you'll train yourself to acknowledge any and all emotions that come out during this time of release.

No emotion is wrong during this sacred ritual, and the more you grasp that, the quicker and easier it will be to release any and all pent-up feelings toward anyone or anything.

Tip 3

Choose Love

When you feel an emotion arising, let it come up without judgement. If you are battering yourself for feeling low, depressed, sad, angry, bitter, jealous, or anything else for that matter, it shames that emotion back into a box. Instead, invite the emotion out, shine love on it, and allow it freedom to express itself.

This doesn't have to take long at all. In fact, you can acknowledge an emotion in a few minutes, and allow it to fully express itself in a beautiful way. Once you do, you'll feel the release go through you. This may come in several forms:

- Tears
- Laughter
- Screaming

30

- Journaling
- Satisfaction
- Ease

The more you practice letting go, the easier it will become. You'll start to create sacred space wherever you go. You may experience a negative situation somewhere, and instead of reacting, you'll go into your sacred space and release it in a healthy way.

This can save a lot of relationships. Why not try it today?

Affirmation

I create sacred space. I am free to express my emotions.

Chapter 4: Forgiveness

During the cycles of the moon is the perfect time to forgive anyone in your life. People will always mess up. If you place someone on a high pedal stool, at one point they will come crashing down. This causes unnecessary pain.

When you walk through the steps of forgiveness it frees *you*. It removes all negative attachments to that situation or person. When you allow freedom to flow, you remove all the past vibes from that memory.

You take back your emotional energy, and you give back to that person their part in the situation.

Let me explain a bit more for you all.

Depending on the type of situation, there will be more energy surrounding you. If someone violated you, abused you, or betrayed you in a relationship, there is a higher charge of energy. I will try to break this down for you in simple terms. Let's start off with the first one.

Situation 1

Violation, Abuse, or Betrayal

If you have avoided the energy of this situation, it may have manifested in different ways. For example: have you attracted men or women who abuse, violate, or betray you?

Maybe they don't outright abuse you physically, but you do put up with their negative emotional abuse on a constant basis.

Do you excuse their bad behavior, because you want to save them?

When violation happens, many souls allow others to control them. They think that control is a form of love. This is a belief system that was built from an early age. If you didn't stick up for yourself in some way, out of safety reasons usually, it will play out in relationships.

Violation is an exchange of energy. If you accepted the exchange, as in blaming yourself for it, (even if it was forced upon you) than you are holding that energy inside of your body, soul, and mind. When you look at the violation as energy, it can be much easier to release.

Let me try to explain better.

It's not just a person who violated you— it was their low-energy. If you look at the energy, not the person, it's much easier to go through the process of forgiving. This person who hurt you was operating in very low-energy, which they chose to force on you. If you were a child, you didn't know how to resist their energy.

As a kid, many situations stick to you, because you didn't understand how to release the energy of your parents, siblings, or other people who may have violated, abused, or betrayed you in some way.

When you hang onto the energy associated with the person, it will continue to manifest in your life. If you give back the energy to that person and release any and all effects of it, it will free you.

Situation 2

Parents and Your Inner Being

Your inner being knows love. It knows what love looks like, feels like, and is supposed to be. If you look to your parents to manifest this love, yet they didn't operate the way you expected them to be, it can cause pain.

Your Inner Being Knows Genuine Love From Mom and Dad

This is why negative emotions formulate, because you understand what perfect love feels like. Here's where I wish to help you. Your parents are also on a journey of uncovering perfect love. They themselves are not fully connected to love, because of their pasts too.

If you can offer love to yourself, where your parents failed, it will help the cycles of release inside of you. Your parents are doing the best they know to do with what they have.

If they haven't chosen the best path, this has nothing to do with you. In fact, you may be a reminder from the Divine to help them get back on track.

Deep inside, you understand that a mom and dad should show unconditional love. This is because that's where you came from. You came from a divine masculine and feminine energy who gave you that. If you ever feel lack of love from those two sources, go to the true source of love.

It will fill you and help you release the anger or sorrow concerning your Earthly parents.

Affirmation

I forgive any and all who have hurt me. I send them love. I connect to my divine source of love.

Pre-ovulation

First Quarter

Each cycle of the moon represents a different stage to your mind, heart, and soul. As you go with the flow of these cycles, you'll uncover the mysteries that may have been

39

hidden from you for a while. There are many resources about releasing during a full moon, but I want to break it down in a very simple fashion for you to grasp.

When people think of a maiden or virgin, in this day and age, they often think the word *naïve*. The thing is, this stage is far from that!

When you tap into your inner Virgin/Maiden, you are tapping into a part of yourself that gets things accomplished. The Maiden is free to do her own thing. She walks in her power, and she knows what she wants out of life.

Picture yourself at an age where you knew what you wanted. You had drive, purpose, excitement, and hope of fulfilling your dreams. That is the Maiden part of you. As many of you grow older, you abandon that part of yourself, and you end up repressing the dreams you once had. Disappointment steps in, followed by a lot of built up frustration.

Here's where I come in. It's time to tap into the Virgin once again. She is a fresh start. This aids in rewriting your negative past and letting go of what no longer serves you.

The Virgin helps you tap into the joy of life once more. She is the youthfulness side to your heart.

During pre-ovulation (when your bleeding has just finished) or the first quarter and waxing gibbous lunar phase, this archetype arises. When this side ascends, this is what will come to mind:

- Purity
- Independence
- Strength

- Uncorrupted nature

- Doesn't answer to anyone

- Authenticity

- Enthusiasm

- Confidence

This phase isn't about sexual status, but rather a state of mind that you tap into. When this phase of the moon or menstrual cycle is happening, you can easily access this side of yourself.

Signs of the Virgin/Maiden

- Juggles projects easily

- Enjoys common interests with others

- Magnetic

- Bold

- Independent

During this phase, you embody the Virgin/Maiden. This is your choice. If you find your emotions feel low, or you often think about what you don't want—tap into the Virgin side of you. Let her magnetic energy pull you into a new beginning.

This phase is not just limited to the moon or menstrual cycles. You can access this part of yourself anytime. Every one of these cycles are present, but similar to how people make New Year's resolutions, their energy bursts forward in that season.

If you feel blockages revolving around this side of yourself, it's time to gently encourage her to emerge. Go back to the side of you who was innocent, full of life, and energetic about your dreams. She is still there.

Here's a few ways to draw her to the surface.

Exercise 1

- Tap into your assertiveness. Be bold in asking for what you want. Ask people to help you.

Visualization

As you quiet yourself today, see the Virgin/Maiden arising from deep inside of you. Picture yourself with complete assertiveness, boldness, and courage to do what you want. Allow that power to flow through your entire body.

Picture a time where you felt completely full of life.

If you don't have a time in your life like that, picture someone you admire. See yourself merging with them. Put on that powerful person and feel how they feel for a moment. Let that boldness seep into your every cell.

Make a List

Make a list of people who could help you with some things in your life. Make it an appoint to ask them for some help today.

Exercise 2

• Put plans down on paper. Think of logical and practical steps for yourself. Of all the cycles, the Maiden uses the most 'masculine' energy in her approach.

Write up a Plan for Your Dreams

Create a list of what makes you feel passionate about life. What sparks you? Write up an easy plan to help you get started.

Exercise 3

• Instead of reacting to your situations, let situations react to you.

Stay in Your Own Power

When a situation pops up, and you feel emotion arising, take a moment to step outside of the emotion and observe what's going on.

Instead of reacting to it, observe it, and allow it to flow through you. Always acknowledge the emotion, but you can make the choice not to react.

Exercise 4

• Rejoice when others succeed. Support other people who are doing well in what you desire.

Visualization

Picture yourself going up to someone who is successful in what you love to do. Give them a big hug and congratulate them with as much sincerity as possible.

See yourself joining hands with others who can help you succeed in what you love to do. Share love between you and others.

Encourage Someone Who's Succeeding

Take a moment and write a message, make a comment, or write a review for someone who's successful. Let appreciation role through you.

By rejoicing over others' accomplishments, it encourages their inner Virgin too. They are being brave enough to express themselves to the world.

Exercise 5

- Watch, listen, and read uplifting material. Allow yourself to move forward with speed in mental, emotional, and spiritual growth.

Dedicate Time to Learn

Create a plan to pick up a book, browse some uplifting videos, or listen to some audio that's going to encourage you. Make a commitment to read, listen, or watch something each week.

Exercise 6

- Let go of anything that holds you back.

Meditate on Who to Let Go Of

If you have a relationship that you know is toxic for your growth, take some time to meditate on how to release them with love.

Whether it's cutting down your time with them, or cutting them out completely, make a clear decision.

Exercise 7

- Come together with people who share common goals, beliefs, or passions. This can help deepen the connection to yourself.

Google

Take a moment today to google some groups, churches, or other forms of communities that can help you with your passions.

Make a choice to connect with a few people. Call a friend, go to coffee, or visit a local place who share your common goals.

Exercise 8

- The Virgin develops her own unique gifts for the world. She expresses her individuality. Invest time, money, and energy into yourself.

Give Yourself Permission to be Unique

Write a letter to yourself expressing how you love your uniqueness. Give yourself a bunch of uplifting words.

Exercise 10

• Dress like a goddess or god. Wear clothes that make you feel active, strong, powerful, and beautiful.

Dress up Time

Pick an outfit that makes you feel good. Spruce yourself up today, and go wild with it.

Exercise 10

• Strengthen your solar plexus chakra. This chakra is where your personal power comes from, as well as your self-esteem. Holding your own power will breed confidence, ambition, and courage to do your passions in life.

Meditation Time

Take a few minutes to do a meditation focusing on your solar plexus chakra. There are many videos you can follow along with.

Exercise 11

• When you're operating in this stage, make sure you give yourself room to unwind. This high-vibration, magnetic, and creative side can make you exhausted. Know when to slow down.

Take a Breather

Find something you know relaxes you. Whether it's a bath, playing a game, or watching TV, find time to unwind today.

Exercise 12

- Do a spiritual practice to enhance this side of you. Try prayers, essential oils (frankincense, sandalwood, rose and geranium) or a meditation to tap into the Virgin/Maiden side.

Find a Spiritual Practice

Everyone likes different things. Take some time to explore what you enjoy doing for your spiritual practice. Browse a spiritual store or read some different books to get a feel for what you love to do.

Affirmation

I tap into my Virgin/Maiden side. I allow myself to go forward fearlessly.

Full Moon

Ovulatory phase

When the moon is full, the Mother cycle begins. For a woman, it's strongest during the ovulatory phase. When you enter this cycle, many things will arise inside of you.

- Nurturing ideas
- Nurturing yourself
- Nurturing children
- Inner strength
- Inner Wisdom
- Caretaking

When you step into this energy it creates a deep connection with Mother Earth—Gaia. As you learn to work with this side of you, you'll understand that it's about your nurturing presence—not control. This deep nurturing is what helps develop and grow those things you've birthed.

You give permission to those little seeds of creation to start the blooming process, and they start their own little journey beside you.

This can be not only with physical children, but in projects, spiritual seeds, or anything of that nature. Letting something thrive on its own two feet is part of being a mother.

Understanding when to let go and when to nourish can take patience with yourself. While the Virgin is about your uniqueness and blazing your own trail, the Mother speaks of attention, care, and presence.

In the natural sense it is taking care of your children, but this is also taking care of your own spiritual and physical needs. You may get impulses to nourish your body, mind, and spirit. It's not to act spoiled, but because you physically need this season of nurturing.

When you take the time to nurture your own needs, it is connecting and healing Mother Earth as well. When you step into the Mother cycle, and you take the time to nurture, care, and love yourself, it makes much deeper changes to the environment around you than you think.

As you step into this phase, make sure you use the energy in a healthy way. Otherwise, it can lead to over-controlling or repression over your creations.

Here's a few ways to draw her to the surface.

Exercise 1

• It's time to simplify your life. What do you need to minimize right now? What are your main priorities you should be focusing on? When you clear out excess, you create space for abundance (in what you desire). The Mother cycle is beautiful and a great provider. She flourishes because she has her ducks in a row.

Declutter

Take some time to declutter something. Look at your schedule and cut out things that aren't aiding your life. Go through a closet, donate some things. This will help clear up space in your mind.

Exercise 2

• Throw a little get together. Invite some people over and make a meal for them.

Take the time to simply enjoy the pleasure of food and company.

Have Fun

Take some time to find a few meals that's easy for you to make for a dinner party. Hash out some ideas of what would be fun to talk about. Plan a few simple games.

Exercise 3

- Take a moment to be present. Allow your mind to fully come into the *now*. Let go of any thoughts about the future or the past.

Meditation

Sit somewhere quietly and connect to your breath. As you do, see all the worries, cares, and things holding onto you dissolve with those breaths. Be fully aware of the present moment. Watch how all those things simply drift away.

Exercise 4

- Create a fun tradition or little ceremony into your daily life.

Write a List of Traditions

Create a little list of something fun to do that'd be traditional. Whether it's Tuesday tacos, gratitude day, or giving people encouragement at the dinner table. Do what you think is best for you and your family.

Exercise 5

- Do you have any practical life-skills you aren't solid in? Such as: changing a tire or fixing something? What skill would you like to learn, but maybe were told you couldn't learn?

Take a Class or Learn Something New

If you think you can't do something, the Mother side will challenge your thinking. She will encourage you to try something new. Challenge yourself today and take a class or learn something practical.

Exercise 6

- Get involved with a community program. Even if it's as easy as building friendships with others, this can bring incredible satisfaction in your life. The Mother side to you needs to continue to nurture.

Look Up a Community Event

Go on a search for a fun, local community event that you would be interested in, or perhaps plan your own! Get together with a group of ladies or men and do something fun to grow friendships.

Exercise 6

- Tap into your resourceful nature. Look around you and see what you already have. Can you use something in a different way that would help you with your current task?

Using Resources

Think about what you need for your life.

Ask yourself the following questions:

- Do I already have the resources for this item around me?
- Can I learn something new to use what I have?
- Do I know someone who can help me with this?

- Can I borrow the item from someone for a while?

Exercise 7

- Lend a hand to those who need help.

Show You Care

Here's a few ideas.

- Buy a homeless person a cup of coffee
- Volunteer at a church
- Visit the elderly
- Offer love and support to someone who's hurting
- Read to children
- Bring treats to animals in a shelter

Exercise 8

- During this phase, don't forget to replenish your own energy.

Self-care

Take some time to show yourself you care. What makes you feel happy, relaxed, and refreshed? Here's a few ideas:

- Take a candlelit bath
- Read a book
- Get a massage
- Do your nails
- Watch a good movie
- Do something you love
- Make your favorite meal
- Listen to soothing sounds
- Meditate or pray

Exercise 9

- Roll up your sleeves and start a garden. If you don't have space for this, there are community gardens.

Go Outside

Go work in your garden or find a local community garden to contribute to. If you can't do that, find a place in nature you love. Connecting to Mother Earth will create a deeper sense of peace and connectedness.

Exercise 10

- Build up your heart chakra. This is the place of emotional depth and love. When it's balanced, it's much easier to give and receive love to others.

Meditation

Find a meditation for your heart chakra. Eat things that are green, and picture green light going in and out of your heart center. See yourself surrounded by love and giving love back.

Exercise 11

- Write down your menstrual cycle. Not just when your body is bleeding, but your emotions, energy, and how much creativity is flowing. This little practice can help you stay in tune with your natural cycles.

Pay Attention to How You Feel

Start a journal or document about your cycle and write down everything you're feeling during that period. Allow emotions to release through an energetic means:

- Writing
- Exercising
- Being creative
- Communicating your emotions

Exercise 12

- Pick out an outfit that's cozy, comfortable, and flowy. Wear something soothing to your body.

Get Cozy

Wrap yourself up in a cozy blanket, wear loose clothing, and nourish yourself today. Maybe wear a soft hat or wrap your neck in a loose scarf.

Exercise 13

- Make something homemade for yourself to enjoy. Put love and attention into what you create.

Creativity

Create something homemade:

- Jam
- Scarf

- Household product
- Shampoo
- Essential oil mixture
- Craft

When you're in the full moon phase, it is a time of clarity and illumination. It's much easier to see what you need to work on inwardly during the Mother cycle. Take the time to feel and fully experience the acceptance, love, and wholeness within you.

When you dote on yourself, you will in turn share that same loving emotion with others. A key to this phase is to embody your own power and be proud of it. If you feel a lack inside anywhere, do the work to restore it back to love.

Affirmation

I love to nurture myself. I love to nurture others.

Waning Moon

Pre-menstrual or PMS/T

The third cycle is what many call the Enchantress, Medicine Woman, or even the Wild Woman. When the magnetic, expansive, creative, and nurturing phase is coming to a close, a shift happens.

During this phase a time of inner work starts to arise. Embracing this phase keeps the cycles in motion, so that you can embody every part of yourself.

This phase is after the full moon, after ovulation, and lines up with the pre-menstrual portion of your cycles. During PMS/T (pre-menstrual syndrome/tension) women may be full of dread to endure this part of their cycle. It can release painful, darker emotions that have been buried.

What if instead of dreading this cycle, you embraced it fully? It's during this phase that things in the unconscious arise to be healed and dealt with. What if you accepted the Wild Woman and went with it?

What can you learn from this phase of your cycle?

This is the phase of the healer—the Medicine Woman—and she understands that you must learn from your emotional lessons in order to grow.

Reflecting on those moments can bring resolve, healing, and freedom. True healing isn't smothering these emotions with a pill or lashing out at everyone. It's a time of self-reflection and restoration.

Committing time, energy, and love to the root of the problem is what will bring complete healing to your emotional, physical, and spiritual bodies. This phase is known to be *wild*, because in order to understand this part of yourself, you have to be willing to take responsibility for all of your emotions.

Many people during this phase point the finger at others for their emotional pain. Instead, embrace the Wild Woman, and allow those emotions to be resolved and healed.

How Do You Let the Wild Woman Do Her Job?

When you're accepting this cycle, first dive in deep by embracing a loving relationship with yourself. Be your best supporter in everything. When you do need external support, be okay with asking for it.

Here's a few ways to draw her to the surface.

Exercise 1

- Take some time for yourself to go within. This isn't plopping in front of a TV. This means spend some quiet time to allow your emotions to express. Without judgement, let them arise, so

72

that you can understand their root causes.

Set Aside an Hour to Reflect

Find a nice, quiet spot, and allow yourself to reflect on the emotions you've been denying yourself expression. Journal, cry, do a little healing ritual, or whatever fits you.

Exercise 2

- Create a safe space for yourself. Whatever this looks like, create an area of your home that is for you to unleash your inner Wild Woman. You could create a sacred prayer space, with memorable items added if you like.

Gather Items That Mean Something

Take a moment today, to gather a few small items that help you feel centered. Here's a few to help:

- Crystals you love
- Sacred trinkets
- Journal
- Candle
- Essential oils (with diffuser if you'd like)
- Blanket
- Plant
- Sign (with uplifting words)
- Pictures
- Smudge tools (sage, bowl)
- Singing bowl

Exercise 3

- Let go of what's overstimulating you.

Time to Let Go

Here's a few things to help your mind settle down.

- Limit screen time (social media, TV, movies, visual games, phone, or books)
- Sit with yourself in silence (or soft meditation music)
- Reflect on your emotions

Many times, putting a screen in front of your face distracts you from your true self. When you busy yourself with other people's problems, you don't have time to face your own.

Exercise 4

- Set up boundaries with yourself and others. When someone needs attention, pen them into your schedule. Don't allow people to demand your time and energy. Give it to them on your terms.

Evaluate Your Relationships

Look at your relationships with a clear eye. Who is demanding a lot of your energy and time? Set up firm boundaries with them, so that you and they both walk in personal power. If someone is using you as their therapist, it's time to take back your energy. Give when you have time, not on their time.

Exercise 5

- When you have children or elderly relatives, it's vital to ask for support, so you can take occasional breaks.

Write a List of Helpers

When you need a mommy break, or a break from any dependent relationships, create a list of people who can help you with that. Some parents will do babysitting exchanges, or you could pay them from a service you offer.

Exercise 6

- When you're feeling extra-sensitive, don't be afraid to ask for support from others. You may need some help at home or a friend's support. Gauge whether you are asking for help to avoid your own truths, or you truly need the extra help.

Who Can Support You?

When you're going through a challenging, releasing period, you may need to call someone to help you. Think of a few people whom you can ask to support you if needed.

Exercise 7

- Eat well to help balance any hormonal spikes. Eat foods high in B vitamins, and make sure you get enough fiber.

Write a List

Write a list of foods that can help you balance your hormones. Healthy greens, veggies, fruits, and fresh fish can aid with this. Listen to your body's needs. If you crave a certain nutritious food, go purchase it.

Exercise 8

- Discover and accept the pain you may have inflicted on others. This discovery can aid in forgiving yourself, as well as those who've hurt you back.

Write a Letter

First, write a letter to someone whom you've hurt. Be sincere and take responsibility for your choices in what happened. Ask for forgiveness and allow the healing words to wash into the letter.

Second, write a letter to yourself. Offer love, compassion, and acceptance to what happened between you and another. Let go of self-blame or fear of facing that side of yourself.

When you go through this process, give yourself love and understanding to where you were at mentally and emotionally. Not that you excuse your behavior, but you can accept your condition at the time. You didn't know what you know now.

Walk through the process of forgiving your past mistakes.

Exercise 9

- Pull your attention to the fifth chakra, which is the throat. This energy vortex helps you speak your own truth. To go through the phase of the Enchantress, you must work through the resistance you put up when it comes to your challenges you've faced. Accepting your actions will help free you. Take responsibility for your part.

Meditation

Do a throat chakra meditation. Speak your truth to yourself and others. See blue light circling around your throat.

Exercise 10

- Nurture yourself. This is a time of deep cleansing and processing, so think about booking a self-care action. Get a massage, go for an energy tune up, or do a spa practice at home.

Set Up 'Me' Time

Be gentle and kind to yourself during this phase. There are a lot of emotions cleansing out of your body, so set up an appointment with yourself. Whether you go outside of the home or not for this *me* time is up to you.

Exercise 11

- Get out in nature.

Go Outside

When you're going through a lot of emotional pain, one of the best cures is nature.

The soothing sounds of the birds, the wind, and the sun on your face can bring healing in a way like no other.

Developing these practices are honoring and nurturing to your own needs. For most, finding the quiet time can be difficult, but once you develop this habit, it becomes easier and easier. When this side isn't allowed expression, it can build up unconscious negative habits that push people away.

These practices are not just for you, but to help all of your relationships in the process. If you're happier, than everyone else around you will feel that joyful energy too.

Affirmation

I allow myself expression. I set aside time to recharge.

Chapter 8: The Wise Woman Cycle

New Moon

Bleeding

During the dark, waning crescent, or new moon phase, when as a woman you are bleeding, is the last cycle—The Wise Woman or Croon. In modern day culture, this phase may be the least valued. She represents aging, loss of fertility, activity, or external beauty.

When you're on your period you may feel slow, tired, gross, or crabby.

The Inner Wise Woman, brings with her physical pain, lack of energy, and the desire to slow down. You may feel you want to introspect, be sensitive, or could experience disorientation.

This phase represents death and renewal. Much like a phoenix bird who loses all her feathers before regaining a brand-new life. This phase happens on different emotional levels in your inner being. In the physical world, your womb is releasing blood, which is a source of life.

This phase of *death* in some ways, is actually happening. On the realm of creativity, this ends a cycle. When this phase is in operation, it shines on the ending of the Wild Woman stage. She transitions the wild, deep, and dark emotions into wisdom.

The Wise Woman is she who embodies the lessons from the previous stage. She reveals to you your inner truth. She is old, wise, and asks for you to be patient with her. She helps you transition into the rebirth once again.

This cycle easily accesses the spiritual realm, and helps you communicate with the sides of yourself you'd previously hidden away. Releasing any and all shame associated with this time of bleeding and death will help this side of you arise in wisdom.

It takes patience, love, and commitment to help this phase take its course.

Here's a few ways to draw her to the surface.

Exercise 1

- Give honor to this dark moon phase. Join a women's talking circle, retreat away, or do a little new moon ceremony.

Gather Info

Look up a talking circle you can join. Gather items to do a small new moon ceremony in honor of the Inner Wise Woman.

Exercise 2

- Find guided meditations and use them during this cycle. Form a bond with your spiritual helpers.

Write What You Receive

After you've gone through your meditation, write down what you've heard, seen, and felt. Get comfortable with receiving information you need.

Exercise 3

- Connect to your intuition. Stretch it, and let the muscle develop stronger. You'll strengthen trust with yourself.

Call a Friend

Practice using your intuition with a friend. Have them ask you questions. Take note of how you feel, what you see, or hear during these practice sessions.

Exercise 4

Use and exercise your energy abilities every day. Clear spaces with sage, incense, or prayer. Bless your food. Value your gifts and abilities.

Honor Your Gifts

Give yourself an affirmation about your gifts. Bless your own energy, light a candle, create sacred space in your home. Bless others. Feel the energy around you. What are you identifying today? Explore your energy senses.

Exercise 5

- Spend time loving and accepting the shadow side of yourself. Let go of the need to judge others or yourself. Express compassion and love.

Accepting and Honoring Emotions

If a dark emotion arises, honor it. Say to it, "I love you, even when you feel this way."

Give that emotion space to heal and feel accepted. Be compassionate toward yourself, and when others react darkly, give them compassion too.

Exercise 6

- Make a choice to love your period.

Give Yourself a Pep Talk

During this cycle, tell your body you are thankful for this time of cleansing. Be grateful for this cycle, so that you can learn how to accept your own inner wisdom.

Exercise 7

- If depression or fear starts to pop up, allow the true message to shine through. Give yourself permission to slow down, reflect, and receive inner wisdom. Trust yourself that you will come out of this cycle with more clarity than ever.

Show Love

If depression is seeping in, tell yourself, *I hear you. I love you. I appreciate you.* Like a wise, old woman give understanding to that side of yourself.

Exercise 8

- Release and let go of old things that hold you back. Whether this is old phases of yourself such as: clothes, collectables, or memorabilia, give yourself permission to let them go.

Go Through Old Stuff

Go through some old stuff you own, but no longer serves you anymore. Give yourself permission to say *thank you* and give it away.

Exercise 9

- Allow change to happen without resistance. This cycle is about transformation. Trust that rebirth will be a result of change.

What Do You Want to Change?

Write down some things you want to change in your life. Can you trust this cycle to help you with those inner shifts? Do you want to be more outspoken? Less outspoken? Cleaner? Friendlier?

Whatever it is you want to change, create a little list, and slowly allow these changes to happen without judgement.

Exercise 10

- Express your wisdom to others. Not that you force your views on other people, but you value your own life's experiences and lessons, so you can help aid other people when they are willing to listen.

Share

If you feel urged to share a story with someone going through a similar situation as you did, share with them. Feel out who needs to hear about your personal experiences.

Exercise 11

- Dive in deep to loving yourself. Look in the mirror, deep into your own eyes, and say, *I love you.*

Create Mirror Affirmations

Take some index cards and write up powerful affirmations for your self-love such as:

- I love you
- I'm proud of you
- You are beautiful
- You are worthy

As you look deep into your eyes, repeat these affirmations daily. You will see powerful transformations.

Exercise 12

- Embrace your looks and age. Your appearance is your personal canvas you are working on in this life. Appreciate every wrinkle, flaw, and part of you.

Body Talk

Look in the mirror and give your body compliments. Instead of looking at what you don't like, admire what you do love about your body. Focus on that today.

Exercise 13

- Pick up some amethyst crystals and put them around your home.

Intuitive

Work with an amethyst, and feel the love oozing off it. Place it under your pillow and write down the dreams you have. This can be clues to what you need to restore.

Learning to embrace the Croon or Inner Wise Woman, can be valuable in your personal journey. You can draw on deep compassion, guidance, and wisdom from her energy within you. Appreciate her.

Affirmation

I appreciate my Inner Wise Woman. I tap into wisdom.

Chapter 9: Men's Moon Cycle

Although the cycles of the moon are very feminine based, men can also benefit from these phases in their life. The cycles of a man are a tad different, but still highly beneficial to understand.

The energy of a man is built up in their seed and the release of it. Similar to women who have blood and feminine sexual fluids.

As a man goes about his life, these fluids build up from substance he consumes. When a man has a *release* of his seed, he goes into the phase of relaxation—just as a woman does during her time of the month.

Have you ever noticed how pent up men get without it? This is resistance to their cycle—just like you'd be ornery if you didn't let your emotions properly flow out.

Men go through cycles during these times just as a woman does. When a man enters the rest phase, a woman must honor his *time of the month* so to speak. While women's cycles are a bit different, men experience these *mini moon* phases, and need that time to rejuvenate.

As a man refreshes himself after his release, honor that cycle and give him time to heal.

Working together to help one another can bring harmony in your relationship. Men also have a feminine side to them, so they can benefit from the stages of the moon just as much as a woman, but as a woman, remember to let your man rejuvenate after he releases his seed.

Affirmation

I allow my man to rest. I give my partner space to heal.

Chapter 10: Honor Yourself

Now that you understand the cycles of yourself and the moon, take the time to honor these phases. Look up a moon calendar for your area and give yourself permission to flow with it. If your menstrual cycle is different from the moon, you can simply honor that cycle instead.

Whether male or female, you all can benefit from learning about these phases. All of you go through emotional releases—every month. It's a matter of becoming conscious of them.

When you give yourself permission to flow within these cycles, you will find powerful energy residing in your life.

What Do You Want to Release?

Identify what you want to let go of, and as the cycles of the moon begin to happen, follow along. Create a journey within yourself to flow with the emotions that are arising.

There may be several layers for you to release, before you get to the bottom of the issue you're dealing with. Don't be too hard on yourself if the same issues pop up again during these phases. It's okay. Allow it to arise and see why you didn't let yourself go deeper in the first place.

What Fear Blocks You?

If you were raised not to fully express yourself, you may have fear blockages as you release things. Let go of shame of having to do it all over again. It's okay. This is why the

99

Mother and *Inner Wise Woman* are important to these releasing processes.

Nurture yourself through each phase, and shine love in every area you wish to address. Let this process become natural for you. As it becomes *normal*, you'll let go of any and all shame concerning how you feel at different points in time.

Give Yourself Time and Love

During each phase, give yourself time, patience, and love to grow. It's okay if you miss a phase, and you feel pent-up about something or other. Start where you're at and grow from there. Be gentle about it all.

Affirmation

I let myself heal at my own pace.

Chapter 11: Relax

When you learn about the moon cycles, it's okay to be relaxed about the entire process. If you feel inclined to follow a calendar or create your own chart, it's completely fine. Following your natural cycle is just as valuable as following the moon's calendar.

Ease

The key I want to point out in all of this is—do it with ease. If you're not ready to enter into a certain phase, be gentle about it. If your Inner Medicine Woman is still struggling, allow the process at its own pace.

I am here to assist you through these cycles of the moon, and in life in general. Remember *everyone* goes through these phases, so you are not alone. Even if it appears some people don't deal with emotional depth, they still have their own cycles to deal with.

If they don't tap into their personal cycles, there will be evidence of it in their daily life. Think of those who have repressed emotions. What generally happens?

The physical body will show them evidence that they aren't listening inwardly. Don't worry about what other people are doing, simply tune into your personal energy.

When You Tune In, You Heal the World

I'm sure you've heard this before, but when you restore your own energy, you heal the world around you. Why is that? Because, you are part of the *whole* of creation. The more individuals that take responsibility for their personal healing, the more the world, as a whole, heals itself.

Understand Yourself

Like I said, go at your own pace. When you understand, love, and appreciate yourself, you will know the cues it takes for you during these different phases of the moon and menstruation.

When you get triggers to *slow down* or *speed up*, it's valuable to listen to those impulses you feel. If your body is speaking to you, yet you ignore it, you will feel it more intensely over time.

If your emotions are rising, but you resist them, again you will feel it in another way. Honor your moods. Treat them with kindness. If you need to retreat, do it, even if for a small amount of time.

Never let others shame you into doing what you feel is wrong for you. For example: if you are in the new moon phase, honor that cycle within yourself. If people are telling you to do the opposite, give love to them, but remind them gently that you understand your own inner being best, and move on.

Tap Into the Energy You Need

With each new stage in life, you may pull on a certain energy more. For example: if you are a new mother, you will pull on the phase of *Mother* inside of you. You'll let her rise with a flourish. Go with the flow. Go where the energy is needed in your current situation. It's okay not to be too strict with the phases of the menstrual cycle or the moon.

Trust your heart to know what phase you need in the moment. Honor each part of yourself and allow it to flow.

Affirmation

I honor the phase I need in my life.

Chapter 12: Moon Ceremonies

There are many types of moon rituals that can be helpful. A simple prayer can do, but sometimes the visual aids can really enhance intention, expectation, and love into a situation.

Here are some of my tips if you'd like to harness your power during a full moon.

Tip 1

Make it Sacred

There are so many things you may view as sacred. A religious item, a person, a memory, or an item in your home. When you do a little ritual to release something, make it special. Treat this time with respect. Honor yourself and what you're doing, and it will enhance the power behind it all.

Tip 2

Gather Sacred Items

Everyone has different items that make them feel happy, cozy, and loved. Gather those items around you and set up a little sacred space to do your moon ritual. When I say the word *ritual*, please don't jump to dark conclusions, because that word has been abused in many ways. You can call it a ceremony or something else if you prefer.

Think of a wedding. There are sacred acts you perform in a wedding such as:

- Exchanging of vows
- Exchanging of rings
- Communion
- Prayer
- Dance
- Throwing a bouquet

- Kiss

All of it is sacred to the couple. It is a tradition that's passed down over time. This is a time for you to let out what you need to. If you need a picture of your mom, a crystal, a bowl of water, paper, fire, or whatever, make it memorable for you.

When you do the act of releasing through the moon cycles, you'll know what ritual is best for you. It may simply be folding your hands in prayer, becoming quiet, and reflecting on your heart. Other people may enjoy writing out what's going on and burying or burning that paper.

It's entirely up to you. If you need some ideas, here's a few mini rituals you could do.

Ritual 1

Candle Lighting

There is something sacred about lighting a candle. So many people light a candle for a passed loved one. Lighting a sacred candle for your ritual can aid you in many ways. It represents your inner flame and can help you remember to keep shining through what you're facing.

Ritual 2

Burning Paper

Writing down prayers, intentions, or things you want to release can be a powerful visual act. As you burn each thing you write (be careful of course) feel the energy of it releasing.

Ritual 3

Focusing on Your Heart

A simple inner reflection can do wonders! If you don't want to pull out anything fancy, simply sitting in a quiet space and reflecting on your heart can help bring an emotional release. During this time, you can cry, laugh, dance, or sing. Whatever works best for you can bring great healing.

Ritual 4

Journaling

For some people, writing their emotions down on paper is powerful. It's a way to sort out what is going on and to get a clear picture of how they feel. If you are someone who responds well to writing down your emotions, this may be perfect for you. You can do all of these rituals together or separate. It really is up to you.

Ritual 5

Affirmations and Mirror Work

Affirmations, confessions, or generally speaking loving words over yourself can enhance healing. If you'd like, keep a small mirror by your sacred space and a collection of meaningful affirmations. Go through them with clarity, love, and authenticity. Stare into your eyes and repeat them with love to yourself.

Ritual 6

Clearing Space

Clearing space can clear the mind. There are many tools to clear the air. You can use these types of things:

- Sage

Sage can be a great visual tool to use to clear the space around you. Light it and gently fan it around the room and yourself. It can have a great healing impact.

- Singing bowls (or sounds that are soothing)

Different sounds impact certain parts of the body with vibration. If you don't own a singing bowl, find a video or recording you can use. As the sound washes over you, see your emotions healing and releasing.

- Cutting cords

If you feel you can't seem to shake a negative relationship, memory, or past experience, visualize the person and see yourself cutting the cord from them. Take back the energy you put out and give them back their energy in the situation.

- Pull out black cords and cut them

Similar to the last ritual, visualize pulling black cords from your stomach and see them drifting away. You could also picture your spiritual helpers aiding you with this. If emotions come out with it, allow them to flow freely.

- Aura clearing

By doing a simple meditation or with a prayer of intention clear up your energy aura. You can do this by picturing a color you feel fits you best. If you know your aura color, even better!

There are also YouTube videos on aura clearing or fluffing that can be helpful for this practice.

- Chakra clearing

The energy centers in the body often get slowed down, so doing a clearing of your chakras can balance many things. In order to do this, you can use a guided meditation, or simply visualize each one of your chakras spinning away any low-energy from you.

If you feel like a certain chakra is more off-balance, put that color around you or consume more food of that color to raise your vibration again.

Archangel Metatron is a great helper for this.

Affirmation

I clear away any low-energy. I am in control of my energy.

Chapter 13: The Final Stages

I want to wrap this up with a few added words. The cycles of the moon shouldn't feel controlling or punishing. Rather let them liberate you into new types of freedom emotionally, mentally, or spiritually. Let it excite you to work with these four cycles.

If you dread a stage, it will only build up more emotional resistance inside of your physical being, which can end up causing a lot of different issues in the body.

When people let bitterness, envy, anger, or sorrow build up, it can cause a disease. This is why I'm offering this information to you. It isn't to control you with the moon—not at all, but to liberate you from things that are already occurring. This is to make you aware of what's going on.

When you bring understanding into a situation, then energy can clear up much easier for anyone. Think of a past issue you've had. Once you understood the root of the problem, wasn't it easier to give yourself love and compassion?

If you find that not a lot of these exercises work for you, that's okay. Give yourself an avenue that brings you clarity. You may simply enjoy releasing burdens in another way, and that's perfectly fine.

Whatever fits you best, do that. As I wrap up my final words with you, little ones, I want you to understand that I am always here to assist you. Although the moon cycles are part of my specialty, there are many other ways I can offer you help as well. As we continue this journey together, I want to share my final sentiments with you through this book.

Offer yourself love every day. Let the moon cycles teach you more about yourself. Let your own menstrual cycles teach you things as well. Be open to learning, understanding, and loving yourself every day.

The more you offer love to your wounds, they heal naturally. Love will always be the most beneficial thing you offer yourself. If you can't seem to understand what's happening mentally, emotionally, or physically, simply offer love to the situation.

It's as easy as that, little ones. Offer love.

Blessings always,

Archangel Haniel

Thank you for reading:

How to Harness the Power of the Moon
with Archangel Haniel

Visit: eepurl.com/cV-Trf for your

FREE

GIFT

Angel Guidance for Wealth

If you've enjoyed this book, I would love for you to post
a review. As an author, I am always learning and growing, and
I'd love to hear back from you.

Come visit me at:

Facebook: Z.Z.'s Angel Card Corner

Instagram: @Angel_guidance11

Blog: www.angelguidancetoday.wordpress.com

Facebook Group: Angel Guidance, Fairies, Mermaids, and Unicorns Magical Realm

Website: https://authorzzrae.wixsite.com/zzrae

YouTube: ZZ Rae ASMR

Other Books by Z.Z. Rae

- Your Voice Your Choice: The Value of Every Woman
- Ties of the Heart: How to recover from Divorce and Breakups (A 12 step-by-step healing process)
- I Want to be a Unicorn (Why Unicorns are Real and You can be One

Angel Guidance Series

- Angel Guidance for Wealth (Abundant Living for Everyone)
- Angel Guidance for Dreams (Your Dreams explained by the Angels)
- Angel Guidance for Inner Healing (Heal your Heart, Soul, and Mind with the Angels)
- Angel Guidance for Creativity (Unlock Your Gift)
- Angel Guidance for Peace (Allow life's burdens to fade)
- Angel Guidance for Joy (Raise your Vibrations)
- Angel Guidance for Energy Healing (Aligning your beliefs with your desires)
- Angel Guidance for Awakening Spiritual Gifts (Uncover your natural ability)

Spiritual Tools

- How to Work with Archangels: (Guidance from archangels for abundance, healing, spiritual wisdom, and more.)

- How to Declutter with Archangel Jophiel (How to Relieve Stress, Anxiety, and Clutter From Your Life)
- How to Work with Archangel Michael (How do I know my life's purpose?)
- How to Find What's Missing with Archangel Chamuel (There's nothing lost in the Kingdom)

Magical Mermaid Messages

- Magical Mermaid Messages on Abundance (How to manifest money with the law of abundance)
- How to Manifest a Soulmate (with a little help from the mermaids)
- How to Manifest a Soulmate Journal (A journal to attract your soulmate)

Books by Natasha House

Grace Alive Series

Christian Romance

- Grace Alive
- Grace Unbroken

Rebirth of the Prophesy Series

Sci-fi Romance

- Fatal Alien Affection
- Fatal Alien Attraction

122

The Jade Series

Epic Fantasy

- The Vullens' Curse
- The Deities' Touch
- The Vision Stone

Super Hero Princess Series

Middle grade/Young Adult

- Zara

Non-Fiction

- How to KEEP Writing Your Book
- Illustrated Sermons for Youth or Adults
- Grace Speaks

Made in the USA
Las Vegas, NV
13 July 2023